WAR IN BRONZE

THE COMMANDO MEMORIAL AT SPEAN BRIDGE

by Iain Gray

Lang**Syne**
PUBLISHING
WRITING *to* REMEMBER

WRITING *to* REMEMBER

79 Main Street, Newtongrange,
Midlothian EH22 4NA
Tel: 0131 344 0414   Fax: 0845 075 6085
E-mail: info@lang-syne.co.uk
www.langsyneshop.co.uk

Design by Dorothy Meikle
Printed by Ricoh Print Scotland
© Lang Syne Publishers Ltd 2014

ISBN 978-1-85217-573-3

Chapter one:

United We Conquer

Dominating the landscape about one mile from the small village of Spean Bridge in the Lochaber region of the Western Highlands of Scotland is a magnificent bronze sculpture of three Commandos depicted gazing towards the grandeur of Ben Nevis.

Known as *The Commando Memorial* and, including the stone plinth on which the sculpture stands reaching a height of 17ft, it is one of Scotland's best known monuments and is a place of special reverence for not only Second World Commando veterans and their families but also for the families of those who have given their lives in more recent conflicts.

Unveiled by the Queen Mother in September of 1952 and located in the heart of the Achnacarry estate, the iconic memorial was designed by the sculptor Scott Sutherland – who won the first prize of £200 in a competition that was open to all Scottish sculptors.

Educated at Gray's School of Art, Aberdeen, Edinburgh College of Art and the École des Beaux Arts in Paris, Sutherland had a particular affinity with the Commandos, with whom he come in close contact while on active military service.

Appointed head of sculpture at the Duncan of Jordanstone College of Art and Design, Dundee, in 1947, he was also a Fellow of the British Society of Sculptors.

There is a memorial plaque to him on the plinth, while following his death in 1984, one of many obituaries paid tribute to him by stating: "He had known and worked alongside Commandos during the war and had a great admiration for them.

"In addition, the scale was right – heroic in proportions – matching the subject. No sooner had the work been unveiled than the greatest possible tributes came pouring in from every corner of the globe.

"The Commando Memorial, despite its remoteness of setting, remains one of the most visited and best loved sculptures in Scotland."

In addition to the memorial, which is a Category A listed monument, there is an equally poignant Garden of Remembrance and an adjoining area where friends and loved ones of those who have been killed in recent conflicts that include the Falklands, Iraq and Afghanistan can scatter their ashes.

Carefully maintained through Highland

Council and with the generous support of other bodies and donations from visiting members of the public, Commando veterans and their families and serving Royal Marine Commandos gather there every November, on Armistice Day, for a special service of remembrance.

The memorial's three bronze warriors are arranged in a V-Shaped 'cutting edge' formation, while inscribed on the plinth is the motto *United We Conquer*, and a plaque that reads: *In memory of the officers and men of the commandos who died in the Second World War 1939-1945. This country was their training ground.*

It was indeed their training ground and, for an explanation as to how this came to be, we have to go back to the dark days of the Second World War – specifically to late May and early June of 1940.

This was when, following a lightning German thrust through the Ardennes, the British Expeditionary Force and elements of the Belgian and French armies found themselves in danger of being trapped in a pincer movement and were forced to seek evacuation from the beaches of Dunkirk.

Thanks to an armada of small vessels that famously set off from British shores, more than 330,000 troops were evacuated and ferried back to

Britain – but the great bulk of their arms and other vital equipment were left behind.

British propaganda skilfully ensured that what had actually been a colossal defeat for the Allies was transformed into the 'miracle' of Dunkirk, helping to bolster public morale.

In a further attempt to boost morale the great wartime leader Prime Minister Winston Churchill instructed his military commanders to draw up proposals for an elite force to carry out assaults on Hitler's *Festung Europa – Fortress Europe*.

He stated: "They must be prepared with specially trained troops of the hunter class who can develop a reign of terror on the enemy coast."

The chilling remit of such a force, Churchill said, was to "butcher and bolt."

Such elite units – later to become famed as Commandos – had already been mooted by the high ranking staff officer Lieutenant Colonel Dudley Clark and, following Churchill's instructions, Sir John Dill, Chief of the Imperial General Staff, set in motion the plans for their formation.

Those who were to become Commandos were initially drawn from serving military personnel who volunteered for what was euphemistically described as "duties of a hazardous nature", or "special service", and also from personnel who had served in what were known as the divisional Independent Companies who had served in Norway and been raised from Territorial Army divisions.

Known as the Special Service Brigade and rapidly expanded to comprise twelve separate units – later known as Commandos – by about the autumn of 1940 its strength had risen to more than 2,000 men.

Every Commando unit numbered about 450 men who were divided into 75-man 'troops' that were further divided into 15-man 'sections.'

The operational structure of the Commandos changed as the war progressed, but it remained under the overall operational control of Combined Operations Headquarters, whose commanders were Admiral Roger Keyes, followed by Vice Admiral Lord Louis Mountbatten and, from October of 1943 until the end of the conflict, Major General Robert Laycock.

A rather bewildering number of Commando units – all with their own specialist functions – were formed throughout the course of the war.

These included the No. 1, No. 2, No. 3, No. 4, No. 5, No. 6, No. 7, No. 8 (Guards), No. 9, No. 10 (Inter-Allied), No. 11 (Scottish), No. 12, No. 14 (Arctic), No. 30 and No. 62.

The largest unit was No. 10 (Inter-Allied), formed from volunteers who had escaped from the

Nazi-occupied territories of Belgium, France, Poland and Norway.

Part of this unit was the No. 3 (X) Troop, later renamed the Miscellaneous Group and comprised of 'enemy aliens' including Jews and other refugees from Nazi persecution in Europe.

Four other Commando units made up the Middle East: No. 50, No. 51, No. 52 and the Middle East Commando, while nine units – No. 41, No. 42, No. 43, No. 44, No. 45, No. 46, No. 47 and No. 48 were formed from the Royal Marines.

There were also the Royal Air Force Commandos, specifically formed to utilise enemy airfields in the aftermath of invasion of enemy territory.

Specialist tasks of Commando units included that of No. 30 Commando, charged with intelligence gathering and even safe cracking.

No. 2 Commando was the parachute unit later renamed the 11th Specialist Air Service (SAS) Battalion and later again the 1st Parachute Regiment, while there was also the Special Boat Squadron (SBS).

Under the operational control of the Special Operations Executive (SOE), which had been tasked by Churchill to 'set Europe ablaze' through covert operations, was No. 62 Commando, also known as the Small Scale Raiding Force.

No. 14 (Arctic) Commando was tasked with carrying out daring operations in the Arctic Circle, in particular the use of small craft such as canoes to sabotage enemy shipping.

Eventually reaching a formidable strength of four assault brigades and more than 30 specialised individual units, those British Army personnel and other volunteers – who also included U.S. Army Rangers – underwent extremely rigorous training at a number of locations in Scotland.

There was the Commando Mountain and Snow Warfare training camp at Braemar, the Commando Training College at Inveraray and, at Lochailort, near Fort William, the Irregular Warfare School.

Commando training had also been carried out for a time in the grounds of the Kelburn estate, near Largs on the west coast of Scotland.

But it was in February of 1942 that Achnacarry became the main training base – to such an extent that the area is recognised to this day as the 'spiritual home' of Commandos past and present and why *The Commando Memorial* is sited there.

Chapter two:
Castle Commando

About eight miles (13km) from Spean Bridge is Achnacarry Castle, also known as Achnacarry House, ancestral home since the mid-seventeenth century of the Chief of the proud Clan Cameron who is known as Cameron of Lochiel.

Both the Achnacarry estate and the castle itself were requisitioned during the war for Commando training and established in February of 1942 as the Commando Training Depot, later known as the Commando Basic Training Centre (CBTC).

By the end of the war in 1945 up to 25,000 servicemen of a number of nationalities had been trained there as Commandos.

In a 30-mile area comprising 250,000 acres of forbidding terrain, mountains and lochs, Achnacarry proved an ideal training ground.

In 2012, in a BBC television documentary marking the 70th anniversary of the establishment of the training centre, Dr Stuart Allan, of the National Museum of Scotland and author of *Commando Country*, said: "The idea of using Highland terrain went back to 1940, and around a dozen Highland properties, including Achnacarry, were used during the Second World War.

"Many of the officers involved had aristocratic pedigrees and they chose the properties. They knew that part of the world because they went shooting and stalking there.

"That was combined with the handy physical attributes of the area: the lochs and mountains. It was about testing individuals to their limits to see if they were up to the mark."

It was Brigadier Charles Haydon who established Achnacarry as a training base, while it came under the command of the First World War veteran Lieutenant Colonel Charles E. Vaughan.

Born in London in 1893 and having served from 1926 to 1935 as a Regimental Sergeant Major with the 2nd Battalion, The Buffs (East Kent Regiment), he was a strict disciplinarian, but was held in great regard by all those who worked with him and trained under his exhausting regime.

In his book *It had to be Tough*, Major James Dunning, who had served as a training officer at Achnacarry, said of Vaughan that: "... his standards for soldiers were set by his long service in war and peace.

"He accepted nothing but the best, whether it be in fitness, training, weaponry and musketry, fieldcraft and tactics, drill and turnout, or even in the more apparently mundane matters of administration such as feeding and hygiene.

"Together, all these factors made the 'whole' – and the self-disciplined and reliant Commando soldier 'fit to fight' and 'fighting fit' with high morale, willing and capable of tackling any military task, under any circumstances, and against all odds."

The recipient of an OBE after the war and instrumental in the setting up of the Commando Benevolent Association, Lieutenant Colonel Vaughan died in 1968, while there is a memorial plaque to him in Kilmonivaig Church, Spean Bridge.

Would-be Commandos were subjected to a gruelling six-week course that began immediately they stepped off the train at Spean Bridge railway station – having to complete an eight mile (13km) speed march, burdened with their heavy kit, to Achnacarry Castle – which became known as Castle Commando, or simply The Castle.

Anyone who could not complete the march within 60 minutes was immediately 'RTU'd' – Returned to Unit.

This speed march has been recreated annually from 1996 by serving military personnel who undertake it to raise funds, through sponsorship, for bodies that include the Commando Benevolent Fund and the Airborne Forces charities.

Strenuous, to say the least, was the training that had to be undertaken at Achnacarry – reflected by the fact that there was a 'drop-out' rate of approximately 30%.

Living conditions were deliberately spartan. Trainees were housed in either canvas tents or Nissan huts and were responsible for preparing their own rudimentary meals.

Day and night, in all weather conditions, they underwent training in unarmed combat, weapons training – including the use of enemy weapons – using live ammunition and explosives and, finally, a simulated but extremely hazardous beach landing known as the Opposed Beach Landing, again using live ammunition.

Speed marches were the order of the day, seven days a week for six weeks, with some of these marches up to 15 miles in full battle-order kit.

Again burdened by heavy kit, they had to traverse a section of Loch Arkaig by zip-line and, pushed to the extreme limits of their physical and mental endurance, were subjected to marches up and down Ben Nevis.

Due to the nature of this punishing training regime there were inevitably casualties, including fatalities, although official figures are not available.

Achnacarry Castle itself even became a 'casualty' when, in November of 1943, a fire destroyed a section of the structure and the roof, all later repaired and Cameron of Lochiel duly compensated.

Writing after the end of the war, Lord Louis Mountbatten said: "I shall never forget the impact Achnacarry made on me when I visited it in 1942, after taking over the Combined Operations Command, and I suspect that neither will those who went through the course, since many told me afterwards they found the real thing less alarming than the Opposed Landing Operation which Charles Vaughan used to finish up each course."

Graduation from what was known as the elite battle school of Achnacarry culminated in the granting of the much-coveted green beret, before those who had survived the punishing six-week training were assigned to their particular Commando units.

In addition to the green beret that they often proudly wore, Commandos were also identified by the other favoured headgear known as the woollen cap comforter – depicted as the headgear of the three Commandos on *The Commando Memorial*, while they are also kitted out in battledress and webbing to carry their arsenals of ammunition.

The three Commandos are also depicted wearing heavy ammunition boots – but on many operations rubber-soled gym shoes, or plimsolls, were the preferred type of footwear, allowing them to move more silently.

Commandos serving in the Middle East were distinguished by their headgear of a bush hat and a cap badge featuring the Mark I trench knife with a knuckleduster as its handle.

The standard issue knife was the iconic Fairbairn-Sykes (F-S), which is depicted on the memorial plaque to Lieutenant Colonel Vaughan in Kilmonivaig Church.

Other weaponry included the Lee-Enfield rifle, the Bren light machine gun, the Thomson sub-machine gun and, later, the Sten gun.

Adding to their arsenal were the Webley revolver and the Colt 45 pistol and the De Lisle carbine – fitted with a silencer for use on stealth operations.

Still in use by military forces throughout the world today, the Bergen rucksack, initially designed to carry explosives and other demolition equipment, was first adopted by the Commandos, while the camouflaged Denison smock, worn over their battledress, also became standard issue for some operations.

Suitably trained and equipped, the Commandos proved a deadly elite force – inflicting blows against the enemy in a number of areas of conflict that included not only occupied Europe but also the Arctic Circle, North Africa, the Middle East and Burma.

Chapter three:
Battle honours

No fewer than 479 decorations were awarded to Commandos during the Second World War.

These include eight Victoria Crosses (VCs), the highest award for gallantry in the face of enemy action for British and Commonwealth forces, 218 Military Medals, 32 Distinguished Conduct Medals, 37 Distinguished Service Orders and 162 Military Crosses.

Other honours, to the Commandos as a whole, include a plaque on *The Commando Memorial* marking the granting of the Freedom of Lochaber to the former Commando Association in 1993.

It was in June of 1940 that the first Commando-style raid was undertaken – by No. 11 Independent Company, a predecessor of what would later be known as a Commando unit.

Known as *Operation Collar*, it was an 'offensive reconnaissance', led by Major Ronnie Tod and carried out on the French coast to the south of Boulogne-Sur-Mer and Le Touquet.

Vital intelligence on German military strength and dispositions in the area was gained, with the only loss of life being two enemy soldiers.

Between 1940 and 1944, nearly sixty raids, all with their own operational codenames, were carried out against German-occupied Belgium, France, Norway and the Channel Islands.

In March of 1941, in what is considered to be the first large scale raid on enemy occupied territory from British shores, *Operation Claymore* involved both No. 3 and No. 4 Commando in a daring attack on Norway's Lofoten Islands.

In addition to destroying petrol dumps, eleven ships and fish-oil factories, the Commandos also captured codebooks and encryption equipment.

A few months later, in December of 1941, men from No. 2, No. 3, No. 4 and No. 6 Commando successfully carried out *Operation Archery*, involving a raid on Vagsoy Island, where the considerable damage they inflicted included the sinking of eight ships and damage to war-related factories and warehouses.

In October of 1942, seven men from No. 2 Commando became the first victims of Hitler's infamous *Kommandobefehl – Commando Order*.

This was, after being landed by submarine in *Operation Muskatoon*, they destroyed the Glomfjord hydro-electric plant in Norway.

The captured Commandos were confined for a time in Colditz Castle before being taken to

Sachsenhausen concentration camp in Oranienburg, Germany, and summarily executed.

The Commando Order was issued to German army and naval commanders in response to what the Nazis alleged were violations by the Commandos of the Geneva Convention – specifically during the Dieppe Raid of August, 1942 and a raid on the night of October 3-4, on the German garrison on Sark, in the Channel Islands.

Known as *Operation Jubilee* and undertaken on August 19, the raid on the French coastal town of Dieppe proved a disaster, with more than 4,000 casualties – mainly from the 2nd Canadian Infantry Division – sustained, although No. 4 Commando managed to destroy a battery of six enemy 150mm. guns.

One of the Commandos, Captain Patrick Porteous, was awarded the VC for his actions during the raid.

Strictly against procedure, a Canadian brigadier had taken a copy of the operational orders for *Jubilee* ashore.

Later found on the beach amongst the detritus of the raid, one of the orders listed was to 'bind prisoners' – although it later transpired that these were orders issued to the Canadian troops, not the Commandos.

It was claimed that bodies of shot German prisoners, with their hands tied, were found after the battle, and this came to the attention of Hitler.

Later, following *Operation Basalt* – the raid on Sark carried out by elements of No. 12 Commando and the British Small Scale Raiding Force – it was claimed that a number of German prisoners, their hands bound, had been shot dead.

Incensed by this, in a note in the daily Wehrmacht communique on October 7, Hitler stated: "In future, all terror and sabotage troops of the British and their accomplices, who do not act like soldiers but rather like bandits, will be treated as such by the German troops and will be ruthlessly eliminated in battle, wherever they appear.

Eleven days later, on October 18, Hitler issued his highly secret *Commando Order*.

With only twelve copies printed and distributed throughout the Wehrmacht higher command by Army Chief of Staff Alfred Jodl, it ordered that captured Commandos should be instantly handed over to the feared and loathed *Sicherheitsdienst* – SD, Security Service.

The order claimed that Germany's enemies had for some time been employing in their conduct of the war methods which contravened the International Convention of Geneva.

It stated: "The members of the so-called Commandos behave in a particularly brutal and underhand manner, and it has been established that those units recruit criminals not only from their own country but even former convicts set free in enemy territory.

"From captured orders it emerges that they are instructed not only to tie up prisoners, but also to kill out-of-hand unarmed captives who they think might prove an encumbrance to them, or hinder them in successfully carrying out their aims."

Describing the Commandos as "sabotage units", the Commando Order stated in unequivocal terms: "From now on all men operating against German troops in so-called Commando raids in Europe or in Africa, are to be annihilated to the last man.

"This is to be carried out whether they be soldiers in uniform, or saboteurs, with or without arms, and whether fighting or seeking to escape; and it is equally immaterial whether they come into action from ships and aircraft, or whether they land by parachute.

"Even if these individuals on discovery make obvious their intention of giving themselves up as prisoners, no pardon on any account is to be given."

Aware that some military commanders would

have severe reservations over putting the draconian *Commando Order* into effect, Hitler ended the order with the stark warning that: "I will hold all Commanders and officers responsible under Military law for any omission to carry out this order, whether by failure in their duty to instruct their units accordingly, or if they themselves fail to act to it."

But despite this warning, some commanders – notably Field Marshall Erwin Rommel famed for his exploits during the North Africa Campaign – refused to relay the order to their troops.

Following the execution of the seven Commandos involved in *Operation Muskatoon*, captured Commandos who had taken part in the *Operation Freshman* raid on the Vemork heavy water plant at Rjukan, Norway, were executed in November.

In the following month, two Royal Marine Commandos were executed by firing squad after being captured in the Operation Frankton raid on Bordeaux.

In April of 1943, in *Operation Checkmate*, seven men from No. 14 (Arctic) Commando used limpet mines to destroy a number of enemy vessels at Haugesund, in Norway. They were all captured and executed.

In July of 1943, the seven-man crew of a Royal Norwegian Navy motor torpedo boat were executed after capture, while following the D-Day landings on the Normandy coast in June of 1944, 34 Special Air Service (SAS) soldiers and also a United States Army Air Force pilot (USAAF) were executed after capture.

Most of them were shot, but it is understood that at least three of them may have been killed by lethal injection while recovering in hospital from their wounds.

In an Office of Strategic Operations (OSS) operation known as *Ginny II*, fifteen American Army personnel were executed in March of 1944 after landing on the coast of Italy.

Arraigned before the Nuremberg War Crimes Trials after the war, General Anton Dresler, who had ordered the execution of the fifteen men, was sentenced to death after his defence that he had been acting in accordance with superior orders was rejected.

With one of the specifications in the charges against him being his role in the *Commando Order*, Generaloberst Alfred Jodl was also found guilty and hanged.

After a war crimes trial held in Brunswick, Germany, General Nikolaus von Falkenhorst, who had been Supreme Commander for a time of German forces in Norway, was sentenced to death for his role in the execution of survivors of *Operation Freshman*.

The sentence was later commuted to twenty years' imprisonment – but Falkenhorst was released in 1953 on health grounds.

Testifying in his defence that the *Commando Order* was a "justified" order, Commander of the German Navy Erich Raeder was nevertheless sentenced to life imprisonment for ordering the execution of the two Commandos captured after *Operation Frankton*.

In common with Falkenhorst, he gained early release on the grounds of ill health.

In March of 1942, in *Operation Chariot*, No. 2 Commando and other Commando elements destroyed the dock facilities at St Nazaire in a daring operation that involved HMS *Campbeltown* and a number of small ships.

The *Campbeltown* was deliberately rammed into the Normandie dock gates, packed with explosives that were detonated by delayed-action fuses.

Of the 611 Allied soldiers and seamen who took part in *Operation Chariot*, 169 were killed.

Sixty-four of them were Commandos, while two of them who survived – Lieutenant Colonel Augustus Newman and Sergeant Thomas Durrant – were awarded the VC.

Elements of No. 1 and No. 6 Commando

participated in November of 1942 in Allied landings in Algeria as part of *Operation Torch*, while Commandos also spearheaded the invasion of Sicily in November of the following year.

In January of 1945, Lance Corporal Henry Harden of the Royal Army Medical Corps and attached to No. 45 (Royal Marine) Commando, was awarded the VC following his actions under fire in *Operation Blackcock* in the Roer Triangle of the Netherlands.

In April of 1945, the 2nd Commando Brigade, as part of *Operation Roast*, was engaged in fierce action at Comacchio Lagoon, northeast Italy.

Their actions – which helped to push the Germans back across the River Po – saved the flank of the 8th Army.

Both Corporal Thomas Peck Hunter, of No. 43 (Royal Marine) Commando and Major Anders Lassen, of the Special Air Service, were posthumously awarded the VC for their part in the three-day action.

Other Commando VC recipients include Lieutenant George Knowland, of No. 1 Commando, posthumously awarded the honour for his actions during the Burma Campaign of 1944-1945 in the battle of Hill 170 at Kangaw.

Chapter four:
Enduring legacy

Although all Commando officers and men served with great distinction and heroism during the Second World War, some particularly colourful characters stand out in the historical record.

Among them are Brigadier Simon Fraser, 15th Lord Lovat and 4th Baron Lovat and his personal piper William "Bill" Millin, better known as Piper Bill.

Born in 1911 in Beaufort Castle, Inverness, and the 25th Chief of the proud Clan Fraser, Lord Lovat was also known as "Shimi" Lovat, with "Shimi" being the Scots-Gaelic version of "Simon."

Commissioned as a second lieutenant in the Territorial Army unit known as the Lovat Scouts, he later joined the Scots Guards. Shortly before the outbreak of war in September of 1939, he was mobilised as a captain in the Lovat Scouts – later volunteering for Commando duty and being attached to No. 4 Commando.

Along with No. 3 Commando, No. 4 Commando took part in the March of 1941 *Operation Claymore* raid on Norway's Lofoten Islands, while a month later Lovat also led 100 men of No. 4 Commando, along with a detachment from the

Canadian Carleton and York Regiment in the *Operation Abercrombie* raid on the French coastal village of Hardelot.

Awarded the Military Cross for his actions during the latter raid, he later led No. 4 Commando in the *Operation Jubilee* raid on Dieppe in August of 1942, and referred to in *Chapter three*.

It was while undergoing Commando training at Achnacarry that Lovat appointed Bill Millin as his personal piper.

Born in 1922 in Regina, Saskatchewan, Canada, Millin returned to his father's native Scotland when he was aged three and where his father became a policeman in Glasgow.

Raised in the Shettleston are of the city's east end, he later joined the Territorial Army after the family moved from Glasgow to settle in Fort William.

Before volunteering for the Commandos, he played in the pipe bands of both the Queen's Own Cameron Highlanders and the Highland Light Infantry.

As 'Piper Bill', he became famed for playing the bagpipes as Lovat's 1st Special Service Brigade fought their way under withering enemy fire from Sword Beach during the D-Day invasion of Normandy on June 6, 1944.

War Office orders were that the playing of bagpipes was to be restricted to rear areas and, when ordered by Lovat to play his pipes, Millin pointed this out.

Lovat, however, who by this time had been appointed a Brigadier, replied: "Ah, but that's the English War office. You and I are both Scottish, and that doesn't apply."

Piper Bill, clad in the same Cameron tartan kilt that his father had worn while serving in Flanders during the First World War and armed only with his *sgain-dubh*, or dirk, then duly proceeded to boost the fighting spirit of his comrades with rousing renditions of *The Road to the Isles* and *Heilan' Laddie*.

Having landed on Sword Beach behind the British 3rd Infantry Division, Lovat's Commandos were tasked with fighting through to Bénouville Bridge that spanned the Caen Canal between Oustreham and Caen.

The bridge – later renamed Pegasus Bridge in honour of the British airborne forces whose shoulder emblem is the flying horse Pegasus – and also the Ranville Bridge over the River Orne, had been vital objectives before the D-Day landings proper of *Operation Deadstick*.

Commanded by Major John Howard, a unit of the British 6th Airborne Division successfully took the bridges following fierce fire fights after landing in the area on the night of June 5 by Horsa gliders.

The task of Lovat's Commandos was to reinforce them until even stronger reinforcements could be brought up from the Normandy landing beaches.

With Lovat, clad in his 'trademark' white jersey under his battledress, his favoured Winchester rifle over his shoulder, clutching a walking stick and accompanied by the pipe-playing Bill Millin—they nonchalantly crossed Pegasus Bridge.

But twelve of his men were killed – shot by snipers through the distinctive green berets that they wore in favour of steel helmets.

Lord Lovat, who recovered from severe wounds he later received while observing an artillery bombardment, died in 1995.

Bill Millin, demobilised from military service in 1946, worked for a time on Lovat's estate and then as a psychiatric nurse in Glasgow before moving to Dawlish, Devon, where he died in 2010.

A set of his bagpipes are now on display in the Pegasus Bridge memorial Museum, while another set and his bonnet and *sgain-dubh* form part of the collection of Dawlish Museum.

In the 1962 film *The Longest Day*, Lord Lovat is portrayed by Peter Lawford, while Millin is portrayed by Pipe Major Leslie de Laspee, who had been official piper to the Queen Mother.

Yet another particularly colourful character involved in Commando operations was Johnny Ramensky, born Jonas Ramanauskas, in Glenboig, Lanarkshire, in 1905.

The son of a Lithuanian immigrant to Scotland and later moving with his family to what was then the notorious slum area of Glasgow known as the Gorbals, he followed his father down the coalmines.

It was here that he honed his skills in the use of dynamite – skills that served him well when at an early age he turned to a life of crime.

His specialities were picking locks and safe cracking, or safe blowing, and he acquired the sobriquet of "Gentle Johnny" Ramensky because he never used violence in the commission of his crimes and robbed business premises rather than private homes.

Despite his skills, however, he was frequently caught and served a number of terms of imprisonment.

It was in 1942, while serving a term in Peterhead Prison, that he was offered a full pardon if he put his criminal talents to use by undergoing Commando training and using his skills to access enemy buildings and headquarters to steal vital documents.

Parachuted behind enemy lines on a number of occasions, he successfully carried out daunting

missions that included purloining top-secret documents
from Rommel's headquarters in North Africa.

One of his most notable feats was blowing
open the safes in fourteen foreign embassies in Rome
– all in one day – after the Allies entered the city.

Duly granted a full pardon at the end of the
war and awarded the Military Medal, he again turned
to a life of crime.

He died in 1972 while serving a one-year
prison sentence in Perth Prison.

Achnacarry, meanwhile, where so many
Commandos were trained during the war, closed as a
training base shortly after the end of the conflict and
most of the units that had served with such distinction
were disbanded.

But their legacy survives to this day, not only
through the present day British Royal Marine
Commandos, Special Air Service (SAS), Special Boat
Service (SBS) and Parachute Regiment, but also the
United States Army Rangers, the French Naval
Commandos, the Belgian Paracommando Brigade and
the Dutch Korps Commandotroepen.

In addition to *The Commando Memorial*,
there are other reminders of their presence in the
Highlands during the Second World War.

The Clan Cameron Museum, about quarter of
a mile from Achnacarry Castle, holds a number of

Commando-related artefacts, while the Spean Bridge Hotel has a small museum that includes memorabilia such as medals and insignia.

During the Armistice weekend of 2012, up to 250 Commandos and their families were invited to the West Highland Museum in Fort William for the opening of a special display dedicated to all those who trained in the Lochaber area.

Cutting the ribbon was Stan Scott, chairman of the Commando Veterans Association – with the association having furnished not only help and advice but also various Commando-related memorabilia.

With the aid of funding from Museums Galleries Scotland, the Heritage Lottery Fund, the Scottish Lottery Fund and the support of a number of other bodies including the Commando Veterans Association, the original display was able to open in the spring of 2013 as a permanent Commando Exhibition.

Paying tribute to those who trained in the area, the impressive exhibition features not only artefacts that include an early Fairbairn-Sykes fighting knife, a Thomson sub-machine gun and even a Commando string vest, but also footage from a film of training at Achnacarry and film of the unveiling in 1952 of the proud and imposing sculpture that is *The Commando Memorial* at Spean Bridge.